23 Storytelling Techniques from the Best TED Talks

Akash P. Karia
#1 Internationally Bestselling Author of
"How to Deliver a Great TED Talk" and
"How to Design Ted-Worthy Presentation Slides"

http://AkashKaria.com

Bestselling Books by Akash Karia

How to Deliver a Great TED Talk

How to Design TED-Worthy Presentation Slides

Own the Room: Presentation Techniques to Keep Your Audience on the Edge of Their Seats

How Successful People Think Differently

ANTI Negativity: How to Stop Negative Thinking and Lead a Positive Life

Persuasion Psychology: 26 Powerful Techniques to Persuade Anyone!

Ready, Set...PROCRASTINATE!: 23 Anti-Procrastination Tools Designed to Help You Stop Putting Things off and Start Getting Things Done

Free Resources

There are hundreds of free articles as well as several eBooks, MP3s and videos on Akash's blog; To get instant access to those, head over to www.AkashKaria.com.

ACKNOWLEDGEMENTS

In addition to TED, I would like to thank Susan Cain, Leslie Morgan Steiner, Malcom Gladwell, Mike Rowe, Dr. Jill Bolte Taylor and Sir Ken Robinson for their inspiration through TED talks.

Finally, I also owe a great debt to Craig Valentine, (www.CraigValentine.com) whose work and coaching has heavily inspired this book.

Without you all, this book would not have been possible!

Thank you.

Akash Karia
Author | Speaker | Entrepreneur

A NOTE REGARDING FAIR USE POLICY

In adhering with the "fair use" policy, I have used limited amounts of copyrighted material in order to comment upon the material and educate the general public.

For educational purposes, I have included excerpts from TED talks. TED, and other graphics, logos, designs, page headers, button icons, scripts, and service names are registered trademarks of TED Conferences LLC. Although I am avid watcher of TED talks, please note that I have no affiliation with TED. This is a book that was developed out of my passion for effective communication and TED talks, and I hope that more people will be exposed to TED through this book.

Finally, throughout the book, I have included links to my website where you can watch the TED Talks referred to in the text. For your easy reference, you can also find the list at the end of the book. I hope you enjoy the talks as much as I did!

RAVE REVIEW FROM READERS FOR "STORYTELLING TECHNIQUES FROM TED TALKS"

"If you are a salesman, or **if you are going to give a speech, you must read this book**. Not only will you learn what to tell your customer or audience in the first 30 seconds, you will also learn techniques that will help you of how and what to tell them in the next 17 minutes so that they will listen to your story and buy it."

— Myster Panama

"This book is very insightful, yet amazingly simple. **These simple changes made to your presentation can transform the boring speech into a fascinating story**. This book has changed my perspective on effective communication."

— Brian N

"**Fantastic!** Many great takeaways to improve my keynotes."

— Tobby Silver

"**An insightful read!** This is a fascinating read with excerpts from stories from presenters at TED. What intrigued me is how the author is able to demonstrate the art used in these excerpts to captivate the attention of the audience. Having to speak from time to time, I was impressed with the styles and tips on how to deliver a talk that will work in holding onto your audience. This book is done well enough that I'll be moving on the other books by the author to gain even further insight into becoming a better speaker."

— Dennis Waller

"**No more boring speeches and presentations**. Who doesn't like stories? A great gift for the presenter who relies on boring power point and mundane statistics. Also, if this describes you, you should purchase this book. An easy read with great direction and ideas."

— Douglas L. Coppock

"**Informative, entertaining** and strung with mind blowing new ideas."

— Tank "Tan Zeek Duwe"

"**Five Stars.** Very interesting, for one who has appreciated the value of TED talks for years."

— Andrew K. Skipp

"Good Stuff, No Fluff! Akash does it again! **Every speaker can put these ideas into practice immediately** – and they should!"

— Dr. Richard C. Harris,
Certified World Class Speaking Coach

CONTENTS

To my loving sister Bintee Karia,

For my life makes a much better story

With you in it.

CHAPTER ONE

THE MAGIC INGREDIENT IN DELIVERING A GREAT TED TALK

What is the secret to delivering a great TED talk?

What is the magic ingredient that makes a TED talk captivating?

TED talks (www.Ted.com) are some of the most inspiring and amazing talks you'll watch. Each presentation is eighteen minutes long, meaning that speakers on the TED stage have a difficult job. They have to distill their expertise and their life's work into only eighteen minutes. Essentially, they only have time to share one idea, which requires them to ask the question:

> "If I could leave my audience with only one single key takeaway message, what would it be? If my audience was to forget everything else I said, what one single idea or lesson would I want them to remember?"

Not only are the ideas that are shared on the TED stage profound, the speakers themselves are some of the best presenters you'll ever see. Unlike the boring, dull, lifeless corporate presentations you hear these days, TED talks are powerful and captivating. They keep you hooked onto every word. The speakers on the TED stage are confident, powerful and persuasive.

So, what is it that makes these TED talks so inspiring?

What are the secrets of delivering a powerful TED talk?

And more importantly, how can you use those secrets to make your presentations more powerful, dynamic and engaging?

To try to answer these questions, I studied over 200 of the best TED talks. I broke each TED talk down in terms of structure, message and delivery.

So, what did I discover?

What was the magic ingredient that made a TED talk captivating?

What was it that made the best TED talks inspiring - which is a word that is often associated with TED talks?

Here's what I discovered. After studying over 200 TED talks, the one commonality among all the great TED talks is that they contain stories. Essentially, the *best* speakers on the TED stage were the ones who had mastered the art of storytelling. They had mastered how to craft and present their stories in a way that allowed them to share their message with the world without seeming like they were lecturing their audience. That's just one of the advantages of stories - they allow you to share your message without your audience feeling like you're preaching to them, which in turn makes it easier for them to accept your message.

In this short guide, you are going to learn how to use stories to make your presentations engaging and inspiring. You'll learn how to craft stories that keep your audience mesmerized. You'll also learn how to use stories to make your message memorable.

By the time you've finished this guide, you will have picked up twenty-three principles on how to create stories that keep your audiences hooked onto your every word. Whether you are giving a TED talk or a corporate presentation, you'll be able to apply the principles used in this guide to make your next talk a roaring success.

Ready? Let's get started...

IN A NUTSHELL

- The one thing that all great TED speakers have in common is that they are master storytellers.

CHAPTER TWO

THE 'STORY START'

How many speakers have you seen that hooked you into their presentation within the first thirty seconds?

How many times have you attended a presentation, and within the first thirty seconds, thought, "Wow, this is going to be good!"

Not many?

Don't worry.

As a public speaking coach, one of the questions I get asked most often is, "What's the best way to begin my presentation? How do I open my speech?"

The opening of a presentation is one of the most important parts of the presentation. If you don't grab your audience's attention within the first thirty seconds, they are going to mentally tune out of it - and it's going to be very difficult to bring them back. You only get one chance at making a first impression, so you better utilize it well.

I have seen too many speakers open their presentations in boring, dull and lifeless ways. The most common (and thus boring) opening is, "Thank you for inviting me. My name is XYZ and I want to talk to you about..." This opening literally *sucks* the excitement out of the room. If your audience members were excited about listening to you, they certainly aren't going to be after that opening!

So, what is the best way to open a speech?

You've probably guessed it: open with a story.

In her great TED talk, titled *The Power of Introverts*, Susan Cain masterfully hooked her audience into her speech with the following opening. I highly encourage you to watch her speech, if you haven't already (watch it here: http://AkashKaria.com/Susan).

Analyzing the effect a presentation has on you is a fantastic way to learn what works and what doesn't when it comes to public speaking. Therefore, as you read the following opening, consider how it makes you feel. Does it arouse your curiosity? Does it invoke any memories? Does it make you interested in the rest of the presentation?

> "When I was nine years old I went off to summer camp for the first time. And my mother packed me a suitcase full of books, which to me seemed like a perfectly natural thing to do. Because in my family, reading was the primary group activity. And this might sound antisocial to you, but for us it was really just a different way of being social. You have the animal warmth of your family sitting right next

to you, but you are also free to go roaming around the adventure-land inside your own mind. And I had this idea that camp was going to be just like this, but better..."

— Susan Cain

INTRODUCTORY REMARKS ARE BORING

Notice how Susan doesn't open her speech with introductory remarks. She doesn't bore her audience with an introduction of herself (the introducer/emcee should be the one who introduces you before you get up on stage). She doesn't bore her audience with gratitude by trying to express how thankful she is that she was invited to speak at TED. Instead, she immediately dives into a story. The best way to thank your audience for the opportunity to speak to them is to deliver a speech that keeps them engaged, interested and involved.

DIVE INTO THE STORY

The reason Susan's opening is powerful is because she dives straight into the story. Starting your presentation with a story one of the best techniques for getting your audience's attention:

"When I was nine years old I went off to summer camp for the first time. And my mother packed me a suitcase full of books..."

The above opening is powerful because:

- **It is different from the way most speakers open their presentations.** Audiences hate predictable, boring openings. If your opening can be guessed by your audience, it's boring! A story is different from the way most speakers open their presentations.

- **It takes the audience along on a journey.** Stories take the audience on a mental journey. As you read Susan's opening, you might have pictured a nine-year-old version of Susan heading off to summer camp. The story had you mentally engaged - you couldn't resist it even if you tried. As executive speech coach Patricia Fripp puts it, "a well told story is irresistible." Stories ignite the listener's imagination, and therefore they give the audience no choice but to be tuned into the presentation.

- **It's relatable.** Stories cause people to search their memory banks for similar, relatable experiences. Perhaps, while thinking about Susan's summer camp, your imagination borrowed details from *your* summer camp. Because the story is relatable, it builds a connection between you and the speaker.

- **People are hardwired to listen to stories.** Stories are the way human knowledge was passed down before the written word. Storytelling is hardwired into our brains. It's the natural way that our brains learn and process information.

So, how you should open your next presentation or speech? With a story. Opening with a story is a tested and proven method for grabbing audience attention and keeping your audience mentally engaged.

IN A NUTSHELL

- Analyzing the effect a presentation has on you is a fantastic way to learn what works and what doesn't when it comes to public speaking.

- If you don't grab your audience's attention within the first thirty seconds, your audience will mentally tune out of your presentation.

- Don't bore your audience with introductory remarks. Begin with a story.

- Stories are powerful because people are hard-wired to listen to stories.

- Stories take your audience on a mental journey. Audiences cannot resist a well-told story even if they try.

CHAPTER THREE

THE SURPRISING ELEMENT THAT MAKES A STORY IRRESISTIBLE

What is it that hooks us into certain stories?

Why is it that some stories have us sitting on the edge of our seats?

What mysterious elements make a story gripping?

If you want to learn how to keep your audiences engaged in your presentation, you must understand this next principle.

The number one thing that makes a story irresistible - that has audience members sitting on the edge of their seats, totally captivated by your every word - is **conflict.**

What do I mean by conflict?

Conflict refers to a fight. It's a fight between opposing forces. A fight between life and death. A fight between hate and forgiveness. A fight between freedom and oppression. As long as there are two strong, opposing forces that make the outcome of the story uncertain, a story will be gripping. It keeps us engaged. It keeps us curious. It makes us ask, "What will happen next?"

A story without conflict is not a very exciting one. If there's no conflict, there's no mystery and no suspense. There's no "What will happen next?". Without conflict, we already know what will happen. We're not curious, and as a result, we're not engaged.

Let me give you a great example. The blockbuster movie, *Titanic,* is a great movie because it contains so many different conflicts. First and most obvious is the life versus death conflict. When the *Titanic* sinks, we're questioning, "Will they live or will they die?" In fact, a lot of the exciting scenes in the movie contain smaller conflicts. For example, during one scene, we find out there aren't enough lifeboats on the ship, so the conflict becomes "Who does and who doesn't get into the lifeboat?"

The second major conflict in the movie is regarding whether or not the two main characters, Jack and Rose, will manage to stay together. Will love triumph or will society separate them because they are from vastly different backgrounds?

Without all the conflict, *Titanic* would not be such a great movie. After all, not many people would pay to watch *Titanic* if all that happened was the two characters met on a ship, fell in love and lived happily ever after. Yes, we would *like* to think that we would be interested in a story without conflict because it wouldn't put us through emotional turmoil, but the surprising truth is that **the conflict in the story is what keeps audience members watching a movie.** It's also what will keep your audience hooked into your presentation.

In her TED talk on *Why Domestic Violence Victims Never Leave,* Leslie Morgan Steiner shares her very powerful personal story. The TED talk is one of the most gripping and powerful ones I've ever watched (http://AkashKaria. com/Leslie). Why is it so powerful? Because the conflict in the story is so strong. Here's part of the transcript from Leslie's speech:

> "Conor used my anger as an excuse to put both of his hands around my neck as and to squeeze so tightly that I could not breathe or scream, and he used the chokehold to hit my head repeatedly against the wall. Five days later, the ten bruises on my neck had just faded, and I put on my mother's wedding dress, and I married him. Despite what happened, I was sure we were going to live happily ever after, because I loved him, and he loved me so very much....It was an isolated incident, and he was never going to hurt me again. It happened twice more on the honeymoon. The first time..."

Wow, isn't that a powerful conflict? When I watched Leslie's speech, I could really feel for her, even though I have never gone through a similar situation nor personally know anyone who has. Yet, I strongly empathized with her because the conflict was so strong - here she was being physically abused by her then-husband, but she can't leave him because she's in love with him.

Conflicts arouse the audience's emotions. Conflicts get audience members rooting for a character, hoping that the character will emerge victorious. For example, Leslie's story unconsciously made me put myself in her position - to imagine what I would do if I were in her situation. As a result, this aroused my emotions. It caused me to share an emotional bond with Leslie. This emotional connection is a must if you want to deliver a powerful talk. When you arouse your audience's emotions, they will have no choice but to be totally and completely immersed in your story.

SHARE A PERSONAL STORY

Another important lesson to learn from Leslie's TED talk is the power of personal stories. Audiences like listening to new things - new ideas, new concepts and new stories. As a public speaking coach, one of the mistakes I see some speakers make is that they use too many clichéd stories.

One of the most clichéd stories that is repeated way too often by amateur speakers is the "starfish story" - the one where a man walking along the beach sees a young boy throwing starfishes back into the ocean. When the man tells the boy, "Why bother? There are so many starfishes you can't possibly make a difference," the boy picks up a starfish, throws it back into the ocean and says, "To that one, I made a difference."

The starfish story is a great story, but the problem is that it's been overused. Audiences are tired of hearing different speakers repeat the same story. It turns audience members off.

So, what kind of stories should you use?

Use personal stories. Personal stories are powerful because:

- **They give the audience new material.** Your story will be new to your audience, which makes it more interesting for them to hear.

- **They improve your delivery.** When you talk about events that have taken place in your life, you will naturally feel some of the emotions that you felt when those events took place. As a result, some of this emotion will show through in your delivery, resulting in a more authentic delivery. You won't have to practice your gestures and your facial expressions because all of that will come naturally when you're delivering a personal story.

As you think about crafting your personal story for your presentation, consider the conflict. Is the conflict in your story strong enough? How can you make the conflict bigger and stronger? Is it strong enough to arouse your audience's emotions? Is it going to make your audience wonder, "What's going to happen next?"

If you answered yes to those questions, then you have a story that will captivate your audience.

IN A NUTSHELL

- Share a personal story.

- The surprising element that makes a story irresistible is conflict.

- The stronger the conflict, the more captivating your story will be.

- Ask yourself, "Is the conflict in my story strong enough? Does it arouse the audience's emotions?"

- The conflict in a story is what keeps your audience curious. The conflict is what makes the audience ask, "What will happen next?"

- No conflict = no curiosity = no interest.

CHAPTER FOUR

HOW TO BRING YOUR CHARACTERS TO LIFE

If you've ever experienced a great speech, you know that it's about more than what the speaker said. It's also about the mental picture that the speaker painted for you. Engaging an audience is more than just giving important information.

Patricia Fripp, an executive speech coach, says, "People don't remember what you say as much as they remember what they see when you say it." That means that your speeches need to help the audience get an experience and create a visual image.

Think about the last great novel that you read. The words on the page created a visual image – you could see the characters in your mind and visualize their actions. A great speech must do the same.

One of my favorite examples of this in speaking is from Malcom Gladwell's TED talk, Choice, Happiness, and Spaghetti Sauce (http://AkashKaria.com/Gladwell). In it, he describes a character named Howard by saying:

"Howard's about this high, and he's round, and he's in his 60s. He has big huge glasses and thinning grey hair, and he has a kind of wonderful exuberance and vitality. He has a parrot, and he loves the opera, and he's a great aficionado of medieval history. By profession, he's a psychophysicist."

— Malcolm Gladwell

Did you see a mental picture of Howard as you read that?

This type of description is what makes Gladwell such a superior storyteller – he really knows how to bring characters to life. He gives you, the listener, just enough descriptive information to be able to picture them in your head.

Speaking is not about "telling". It's more about "showing" the audience so that they get an experience that really sinks in. Gladwell always follows the principle of showing rather than just telling.

For example, he goes on to talk about Howard and says Howard, "has a parrot, and he loves the opera, and he's a great aficionado of medieval history." So now you can picture what Howard looks like and you also know that he's a little bit of a quirky guy. He could have said, "Howard is a quirky guy," but that wouldn't have given you the same understanding of the essence of this character.

When you're writing your own speech, you want to apply this principle. Providing this type of sensory detail that's very specific and visual about the characters in your speeches will help them to come alive for the audience. This is the principle of "showing" instead of "telling".

IN A NUTSHELL

- It's important to bring your characters alive by providing details about the way they look

- You always want to give your audience sensory information that allows them to create a mental image of your characters

- Always follow the principle of "showing" instead of "telling"

CHAPTER FIVE

HOW TO CREATE MENTAL MOTION PICTURES FOR YOUR AUDIENCE

There are five senses that we use to experience the world – sight, sound, touch, smell, and taste. By providing descriptions that use as many of these senses as possible, you can help your audience to create a mental motion picture of your characters and stories.

Let's look at an example of this from Mike Rowe. He's the host of the popular Discovery Channel series "Dirty Jobs". In his speech titled "Learning from Dirty Jobs" (http://AkashKaria.com/Mike) he recounts an experience with the job of castrating sheep. He says:

"In the space of about two seconds, Albert had the knife between the cartilage of the tail, right next to the butt of the lamb, and very quickly the tail was gone and in the bucket that I was holding. A second later, with a big thumb and a well calloused forefinger, he had the scrotum firmly in his grasp. And he pulled it toward him, like so, and he took the knife and he put it on the tip. Now you think you know what's coming, Michael -- you don't, OK? He snips it, throws the tip over his shoulder, and then grabs the scrotum and pushes it upward, and then his head dips down, obscuring my view, but what I hear is a slurping sound, and a noise that sounds like Velcro being yanked off a sticky wall..."

— Mike Rowe

How did that description make you feel? Were you grossed out by it? Did you make a face of disgust the way that I did when I heard it?

Could you picture the story in your mind like a movie? What about that short description was so powerful?

The true power of this type of story is that it provides the audience with a wealth of sensory information to make it come alive. You can visualize what's happening like a motion picture inside your mind's eye.

Using most or all of the five senses in your talks will help you to do this. Those senses include:

- Visual (sight)

- Auditory (sound)

- Kinesthetic (touch, emotions)

- Olfactory (smell)

- Gustatory (taste)

When referring to all of them, we'll use the acronym VAK-OG. Let's look at how Mike Rowe enlisted your senses in this talk:

Visual – What could you see in that short story? Could you visualize the knife and the man holding the sheep's scrotum with his "big thumb and well-calloused forefinger"?

Auditory – What sounds could you hear? The one that stands out to me is the tearing sound of "Velcro being yanked off a sticky wall."

Kinesthetic – What could you feel? There were references to "firmly holding" the sheep's scrotum. And you might have even gone to a place where you could imagine the pain the sheep was experiencing.

Olfactory – What could you smell? This passage doesn't reference any particular smells, but you might begin to imagine the smell of livestock on a farm if that's something with which you're familiar.

Gustatory – What could you taste? Again, there's no specific description of taste but this description might have left a bad taste in your mouth!

By combining many sensual aspects in his story, Mike Rowe was able to help you create a mental movie of the experience. Eric Whitman, in his book *Cashvertising*, writes:

> "Any time we experience anything in life, a blend of these elements is always present. We call these elements "IRs" – internal representations – because they represent our experience of the world around us internally, in our heads.
>
> In fact, memory is just a blend of these elements. Whenever you recall any experience, whether it's a the pizza you a yesterday, or the roller coaster you screamed on 28 years ago, you're accessing a blend of these five elements; a set pattern that "equals" your experience."

In other words, blending the elements of the five senses helps to bring your story to life and internalize it for the audience. As a result, your speech will be more powerful and impactful to your audience.

As you can see from the examples covered so far in this chapter, you don't need to make your descriptions long and incredibly detailed. But you do need to hit on as many of the five senses as possible in order to create a great experience for your audience.

IN A NUTSHELL

It's important that you use the senses of VAKOG when constructing your speech. Include as many senses as possible.

- Visual – What can you see?

- Auditory – What can you hear?

- Kinesthetic – What can you feel – either physically or emotionally?

- Olfactory – What could you smell?

- Gustatory – What could you taste?

- Even though you need to include some detail, remember to keep your descriptions short

CHAPTER SIX

ADDING INTERNAL CREDIBILITY TO YOUR STORIES USING SPECIFICITY

When crafting your personal story, it's important to keep in mind that you need to provide as many specific details as possible. In order to turn your story into a mental movie for your audience, provide audience members with as many specific details as possible. For example, instead of saying, "The man was tall," say "He was about 6 foot 5 inches." Instead of saying, "I was speaking to a large group of people," say "I was speaking to a group of 500 CEOs."

Do you see how the specific details help your audience see the scene? Non-specific statements such as "the man was tall" don't help your audience members picture the characters and the scene in their mind. Saying, "He was about 6 foot 5, with ripped muscles" provides enough detail for your audience to be able to *see* the characters and the scene.

Also, according to research that I highlight in my book, *How to Deliver a Great TED Talk*, adding very specific details to your talk increases the internal credibility of your presentation.

For example, consider the following section from Leslie Morgan Steiner's speech (http://AkashKaria.com/Leslie):

> "Conor used my anger as an excuse to put both of his hands around my neck and to squeeze so tightly that I could not breathe or scream, and he used the chokehold to hit my head repeatedly against the wall. Five days later, the ten bruises on my neck had just faded..."

Notice how, instead of saying "A couple of days later," Leslie says "five days later." First, this gives the audience a concrete timeline of the events. Second, it adds credibility to the story.

Let's take another example from a great TED talk by Dr. Jill Bolte Taylor. In her TED talk, *Stroke of Insight* (http://AkashKaria.com/Jill/) Dr. Taylor says:

> "But on the morning of December 10, 1996, I woke up to discover that I had a brain disorder of my own."

Do you notice how much more powerful that is than saying, "But one morning a couple of years ago, I woke up to discover I had a brain disorder of my own"? Doesn't giving the specific date - December 10, 1996 - sound more believable than saying, "a couple of years ago"?

When crafting your story, avoid non-specific language. Provide specific details about the characters, scenes and dates. The specific details will help your audience *see* what you're saying, as well as add internal credibility to your presentation.

IN A NUTSHELL

- Specific details help your audience see what you're saying.

- Specificity adds internal credibility to your presentation.

- Always provide specific details about characters, scenes and dates.

CHAPTER SEVEN

THE POWER OF POSITIVE STORIES

There are two types of stories you can share with your audience: "positive-message" stories and "negative-message" stories. Here's what I mean.

Positive-message stories are stories where the main character manages to overcome the conflict. The character changes for the better as a result of having overcome the conflict. This type of story shows the audience what they *should* do and leaves them in high spirits.

As an example of a positive-message story, think of a typical rags-to-riches story. One of my favorite movies is The *Pursuit of Happyness*, starring Will Smith. Based on a true story, Will Smith plays the role of Chris Gardner. Chris Gardner has invested most of his money on a device called a bone density scanner. However, he is unable to sell the devices and ends up losing his house and his wife. He is forced to live on the streets with his son. (Side note: This is the conflict: Will they survive or perish? Will Chris be able to take care of his son or will he lose his son too? How will they overcome the difficulty?)

However, through sheer determination and hard work, Chris ends up with an unpaid six-month internship as a stockbroker. His effort pays off, he ends up with a full-time employment offer as a stockbroker, and by the end of the movie, through his hard work, he has formed his own multimillion-dollar brokerage firm.

The Pursuit of Happyness is a positive-message story because it shares with the audience a positive message - that through hard work and persistence, we can overcome even the most difficult challenges we face in life. The end of the story leaves the audience on an emotional high.

The negative-message story, as you can guess, is one where the character *doesn't* manage to overcome the conflict and in fact, ends up in a worse state than before. This is what I call a negative-message story because it teaches the audience what *not* to do. While the story may be instructive, it is not inspiring. It leaves audiences on an emotional low, which is generally not how you want to end your presentation.

Positive-message stories are inspiring. They leave audiences on an emotional high. Negative-message stories are instructive but they leave audiences on an emotional low.

Whenever possible, share positive-message stories with your audience. Through the positive-message story, you will be able to educate as well as inspire your audience. The positive-message story allows you to share a motivational message with your audience without being perceived as someone who is shoving advice down their throats.

As an example of a positive message story, let's examine part of a TED talk by Sir Ken Robinson. In his great TED talk on *How Schools Kill Creativity* (http://AkashKaria.com/Ken), Sir Ken uses the following positive-message story:

> I'm doing a new book at the moment called "Epiphany," which is based on a series of interviews with people about how they discovered their talent. I'm fascinated by how people got to be there. It's really prompted by a conversation I had with a wonderful woman who maybe most people have never heard of; she's called Gillian Lynne -- have you heard of her? Some have. She's a choreographer and everybody knows her work. She did "Cats" and "Phantom of the Opera." She's wonderful. I used to be on the board of the Royal Ballet in England, as you can see. Anyway, Gillian and I had lunch one day and I said, "Gillian, how'd you get to be a dancer?" And she said it was interesting; when she was at school, she was really hopeless. And the school, in the '30s, wrote to her parents and said, "We think Gillian has a learning disorder." She couldn't concentrate; she was fidgeting. I think now they'd say she had ADHD. Wouldn't you? But this was the 1930s, and ADHD hadn't been invented at this point. It wasn't an available condition. (Laughter) People weren't aware they could have that.

Anyway, she went to see this specialist. So, this oak-paneled room, and she was there with her mother, and she was led and sat on this chair at the end, and she sat on her hands for 20 minutes while this man talked to her mother about all the problems Gillian was having at school. And at the end of it -- because she was disturbing people; her homework was always late; and so on, little kid of eight -- in the end, the doctor went and sat next to Gillian and said, "Gillian, I've listened to all these things that your mother's told me, and I need to speak to her privately." He said, "Wait here. We'll be back; we won't be very long," and they went and left her. But as they went out the room, he turned on the radio that was sitting on his desk. And when they got out the room, he said to her mother, "Just stand and watch her." And the minute they left the room, she said, she was on her feet, moving to the music. And they watched for a few minutes and he turned to her mother and said, "Mrs. Lynne, Gillian isn't sick; she's a dancer. Take her to a dance school."

I said, "What happened?" She said, "She did. I can't tell you how wonderful it was. We walked in this room and it was full of people like me. People who couldn't sit still. People who had to move to think." Who had to move to think. They did ballet; they did tap; they did jazz; they did modern; they did contemporary. She was eventually auditioned for the Royal Ballet School; she became a soloist; she had a wonderful career at the Royal Ballet. She eventually graduated from the Royal Ballet School and founded her own company -- the Gillian Lynne Dance Company -- met Andrew Lloyd Weber. She's been responsible for some of the most successful musical theater productions in history; she's given pleasure to millions; and she's a multi-millionaire. Somebody else might have put her on medication and told her to calm down. (audience applause)

At the end of the story, Sir Ken Robinson received a rousing round of applause from the audience. Why? Because the story left them on an emotional high.

THE POWER OF DIALOGUE IN STORYTELLING

Another important lesson to learn from Sir Ken Robinson is the importance of dialogue in storytelling. Throughout the above story, he uses dialogue. Here's an example:

And they watched for a few minutes and he turned to her mother and said, "Mrs. Lynne, Gillian isn't sick; she's a dancer. Take her to a dance school."

Now here's the same in narration:

"And they watched for a few minutes and the doctor told Gillian's mother that her daughter wasn't sick. She was a dancer and that she should be taken to dance school."

Do you *feel* the difference between dialogue and narration?

Dialogue is more powerful than narration. It puts audience members into the scene, allowing them to hear exactly what was said. Dialogue is also shorter and punchier than narration. Finally, another advantage of dialogue is that it allows you to use vocal variety - to slightly change the pace, pitch and volume of your voice to reflect the emotions and speech of the different characters in your speech. As a result, your delivery will be more dynamic and engaging.

When delivering your story, always use dialogue - not narration.

IN A NUTSHELL

- Positive-message stories are inspiring.

- Leave your audience on an emotional high.

- Use dialogue, not narration.

CHAPTER EIGHT

THE SPARK, THE CHANGE AND THE TAKEAWAY

We know that the conflict in a story is what makes it exciting. And we also know that positive-message stories are what inspires an audience.

Between the conflict and the final victory of the character, we have what I refer to as the "spark." The spark refers to the process, idea or wisdom that allows the character to overcome the conflict.

The spark is one of the most valuable parts of the story. It's the process or the wisdom that audience members can take home with them and use to overcome similar conflicts in their own lives.

Think about a time that you faced a difficult challenge in your life. How did you overcome it? What was the process you used to overcome the conflict? What was the wisdom that allowed you to push past the difficulty?

Let me give you a simple example. Imagine a man - we'll call him John - who is 300 pounds overweight.

[Conflict/Difficulty]: John *wants* to lose weight, but every time he goes on a diet, he gives up quickly because his commitment is not strong enough. As a result, he's depressed.

[The Spark]: When he goes to the doctor for his yearly checkup, the doctor tells him, "John, if you don't lose weight, you'll be dead in five years." This is the spark that John needs to change his life.

[The Change] Fast forward to a year later, and John has lost over 250 pounds and is living a happier life.

[The takeaway]: If you *want* to achieve your goal, but don't *commit* to it and don't have a strong reason for achieving it, then you'll never achieve it.

The above story is very simple, but I've made it simple to explain several critical storytelling concepts to you:

1. **The Spark**: The spark is the wisdom or the process that the character in your story receives in order to overcome the conflict.

    In one of my stories, I talk about a time I was very excited about starting up my own business. However, one of my friends was very negative and kept on reminding me that I wouldn't be successful because I didn't have enough experience. Whenever I talked about my business, my friend would shoot down my ideas with her negativity. As a result, I struggled with thoughts of not being good enough to start a business.

The spark that allowed me to get over my friend's negativity was a quotation by Eleanor Roosevelt. It was: "No one can make you feel inferior without your consent." It was then I realized that I had given my friend permission to make me feel inferior - and at that moment in time, I made a conscious decision to not let her negativity pull me down.

What was the spark that caused you to overcome the conflict you were facing in your life? Perhaps it was a quotation you read, or advice you received from a mentor or a technique you learned from a book. Share the spark with your audience and perhaps it might just be what they need to help them overcome the challenges they may be facing.

2. **The Change**. Characters must change as a result of the conflict. There has to be a difference in the character - either the character's circumstances or his/her personality - because of having overcome the conflict. For example, in the weight loss story about John, John went from being overweight to being a thinner, healthier person.

3. **The Takeaway.** Each story must have a key takeaway message. Bill Gove, the first president of the National Speakers Association, wisely said to be a great public speaker you need to, "Tell a story

and make a point." What's the point of your story? What's the key takeaway message of your speech? Summarize your key message in a short, memorable phrase so that your audience will remember and repeat it.

If I had to simplify the structure of a great story, here's what it would look like:

Character --> Conflict --> Spark --> Change in Character --> Takeaway Message

Let's have a look at an example of this process. We'll use Leslie Morgan Steiner's TED talk on domestic violence to look at the above structure in action. Watch Leslie's speech here (http://AkashKaria.com/Leslie), and then we will examine the characters, conflict, spark, change and takeaway message in the speech.

Ready?

Who are the characters in Leslie's speech? The two characters in Leslie's speech are Leslie and her ex-husband. Since Leslie is standing on stage, we don't need any description of her. What about her ex-husband? What information do we have about him? Leslie tells us that her ex-husband, Conor, "had just graduated from an Ivy League school, and that he worked at a very impressive Wall Street bank ... he was smart and funny and he looked like a farm boy. He had these big cheeks, these big apple cheeks and this wheat-blond hair, and he seemed so sweet." Leslie gives us enough information about Conor to create a mental image of him in our heads.

When telling stories in your speeches and presentations, make sure that you provide some specific details about how your main characters look.

What's the conflict in Leslie's story?

> "Conor used my anger as an excuse to put both of his hands around my neck as and to squeeze so tightly that I could not breathe or scream, and he used the chokehold to hit my head repeatedly against the wall. Five days later, the ten bruises on my neck had just faded, and I put on my mother's wedding dress, and I married him. Despite what happened, I was sure we were going to live happily ever after, because I loved him, and he loved me so very much....It was an isolated incident, and he was never going to hurt me again. It happened twice more on the honeymoon. The first time..."

The conflict in Leslie's story is that she is being physically abused by her then-husband but can't leave him because she's in love with him and keeps believing that he will change.

What's the spark in Leslie's story?

> "I was able to leave, because of one final, sadis-

tic beating that broke through my denial. I realized that the man who I loved so much was going to kill me if I let him. So I broke the silence. I told everyone: the police, my neighbors, my friends and family, total strangers..."

The cure is that Leslie finds the courage to leave Conor because of one final beating which broke through her denial.

How does the main character in the story change as a result of the conflict? In Leslie's story, the change is that she goes from being in an abusive relationship to finally getting out of it. She goes from being in denial about her situation to finally accepting that the man she loved so much was going to kill her. Furthermore, she goes from keeping her abusive relationship a secret to sharing her story with the world so that she can help others in similar situations.

Finally, what is the takeaway message of Leslie's story? What lesson does she leave the audience with? Leslie uses her story to take us through the different steps of a domestic violence relationship, but the final takeaway message for her audience is that instead of blaming victims of violent relationships for staying in those relationships, we should (as she says) "recast survivors as wonderful, loveable people with full futures. Recognize the early signs of violence and conscientiously intervene, de-escalate it, [and] show victims a safe way out."

The storytelling structure you've learned in this book may be simple, but it's powerful. It's proven to work time and time again, so use it to make your presentation engaging and interesting!

IN A NUTSHELL

- Your story must contain the spark that allowed your character to overcome the conflict.

- Show the change in your character.

- Leave your audience with your key takeaway message.

CHAPTER NINE

WRAP UP

The magic ingredient in all great TED talks is storytelling. If you master the art of storytelling, you'll be able to keep your audiences captivated Whether you're giving a TED talk or a corporate presentation, use stories in your presentations because stories are powerful. Stories are inherently interesting. They're memorable. And they can turn any boring presentation in a brilliant one.

Use the following twenty-three principles covered in this guide to make your next presentation an outstanding success:

1. Watch videos of great speakers. Analyzing the effect a presentation has on you is a fantastic way to learn what works and what doesn't when it comes to public speaking.

2. If you don't grab your audience's attention within the first thirty seconds, your audience will mentally tune out of your presentation.

3. Don't bore your audience with introductory remarks. Begin with a story.

4. Stories are powerful because people are hardwired to listen to stories.

5. Stories take your audience on a mental journey. Audiences cannot resist a well-told story even if they try.

6. Share a personal story.

7. The surprising element that makes a story irresistible is conflict. The stronger the conflict, the more captivating your story will be.

8. Ask yourself, "Is the conflict in my story strong enough? Does it arouse my audience's emotions?"

9. No conflict = no curiosity = no interest.

10. Bring your characters alive by providing details about their appearance.

11. Give your audience enough sensory information to construct a mental image of your main characters.

12. Show, don't tell.

13. Turn your scenes into mental movies using the VAKS.

14. Pack in as many of the senses as possible but keep your descriptions short.

15. Provide specific detail because it helps your audience see what you're saying.

16. Specificity adds internal credibility to your presentation.

17. Positive-message stories are inspiring. They allow you to share your message with your audience without lecturing them.

18. Leave your audience on an emotional high.

19. Use dialogue, not narration. Dialogue is shorter and more impactful than narration, and also allows you to use vocal variety in your delivery.

20. Your story should contain the spark that allowed your character to overcome the conflict.

21. Show the change in the character as a result of the conflict.

22. Wrap up your story by leaving your audience with a final takeaway message.

23. Make your takeaway message short so that your audience can remember and repeat it.

LIST OF TED TALKS MENTIONED IN THE BOOK

For your reference, here's a quick list of the TED talks mentioned in this book (in order of 'appearance'):

The Power of Introverts by Susan Cain
http://AkashKaria.com/Susan

Why Domestic Violence Victims Never Leave by Leslie Morgan Steiner
http://AkashKaria.com/Leslie

Choice, Happiness, and Spaghetti Sauce by Malcom Gladwell
http://AkashKaria.com/Gladwell

Learning from Dirty Jobs, by Mike Rowe
http://AkashKaria.com/Mike

Stroke of Insight, by Dr. Jill Bolte Taylor
http://AkashKaria.com/Jill

How Schools Kill Creativity by Sir Ken Robinson
http://AkashKaria.com/Ken

QUESTIONS OR COMMENTS?

I'd love to hear your thoughts. Email me at: akash.speaker@gmail.com

INTERESTED IN HAVING ME SPEAK AT YOUR NEXT EVENT?

I deliver high-impact keynotes and workshops on productivity, time-management, success psychology and effective communication. Check out the full list of my training programs on http://AkashKaria.com/keynotes/ and reach me on akash.speaker@gmail.com to discuss how we can work together.

GRAB $297 WORTH OF FREE RESOURCES

Want to learn the small but powerful hacks to make you insanely productive? Want to discover the scientifically proven techniques to ignite your influence? Interested in mastering the art of public speaking and charisma? Then head over to http://www.AkashKaria.com to grab your free "10X Success Toolkit" (free MP3s, eBooks and videos designed to unleash your excellence). Be sure to sign up for the newsletter and join over 11,800 of your peers to receive free, exclusive content that I don't share on my blog.

YOU MIGHT ALSO ENJOY

If you enjoyed this book, then check out Akash's other books (and see what other readers are saying).

HOW TO DESIGN TED-WORTHY PRESENTATION SLIDES

The Phenomenal No.1 Amazon Bestseller

"A great resource...I have been teaching workshops at universities and Fortune 500 Campuses up and down the East Coast on building better presentations. Akash hits all the right notes in this book. A must read for anyone wanting to build powerful presentations."

— David Bishop

"I will admit to rarely reviewing books. However, this book was such a step above any others I've read on the art of PowerPoint presentations, I had to give it a five star review. I have already recommended this book on my blog and will keep it in my ready reference...!"

— David Schwind

Get the book on Amazon: http://AkashKaria.com/ TEDPresentation/

HOW TO DELIVER A GREAT TED TALK: PRESENTATION SECRETS OF THE WORLD'S BEST SPEAKERS

"Why can some speakers grab the attention of an audience and keep them spellbound throughout their entire presentation, but most fall flat on their faces and are quickly forgotten? Akash has captured the best ideas, tools, and processes used by some of the best speakers and presenters in the world. *He has distilled them in to a step-by-step, easy-to-read guide that will help you discover, develop, and deliver presentations which help you stand out from the crowd… Whether you are a new speaker learning the art of speaking, or a veteran looking for a new perspective, How to Deliver* a Great TED Talk is a wise investment that can help take your speaking to a higher level."

— Michael Davis, Certified World Class Speaking Coach

"I waited quite a while to read this book, and now that I have, I wish I would have opened it sooner. Fantastic information and easy to follow format."

— Noell Beadelia

Get the book on Amazon: http://AkashKaria.com/ TEDTalkBook/

READY, SET...PROCRASTINATE! 23 ANTI-PROCRASTINATION TOOLS DESIGNED TO HELP YOU STOP PUTTING THINGS OFF AND START GETTING THINGS DONE

"This is one book you should not delay reading! Having struggled with procrastination for much of my life, Akash Karia's book came like a breath of fresh air. He provides clear, practical advice on how to overcome the problem, but warns that you will need to work at it daily. This is a quick, very useful read and with 23 tips on offer, there will be several that you can identify with and implement for immediate results. If there is just one thing that you should not put off, it is reading this book."

— Gillian Findlay

Get the book on Amazon: http://AkashKaria.com/Anti-Procrastination/

ANTI NEGATIVITY: HOW TO STOP NEGATIVE THINKING AND LEAD A POSITIVE LIFE

"Akash is a master at taking complex ideas and communicating with simplicity and brilliance. He honors your time by presenting what you need to know right away, and follows up with some excellent examples as reinforcement. If you're looking for some simple and

effective ways to stop thinking negatively and a new season of positivity, definitely check out this book."
— Justin Morgan

Get the book on Amazon: http://AkashKaria.com/Anti-Negativity/

PERSUASION PSYCHOLOGY: 26 POWERFUL TECHNIQUES TO PERSUADE ANYONE!

"I'm a huge fan of Akash's writing style and the way he can distill quite a complex subject into concise bite-sized points you can take away and convert into action. The book covers many different aspects of persuasion from the way you look to the words you use."

— Rob Cubbon, author of "From Freelancer to Entrepreneur"

Get the book on Amazon: http://AkashKaria.com/Persuasion/

WANT MORE?

Then check out Akash's author-page on Amazon: http://bit.ly/AkashKaria.

ABOUT THE AUTHOR

Akash Karia is an award winning speaker and peak-productivity coach who has been ranked as one of the Top Ten speakers in Asia Pacific. He is an in-demand international speaker who has spoken to a wide range of audiences including bankers in Hong Kong, students in Tanzania, governmental organizations in Dubai and yoga teachers in Thailand. He currently lives in Tanzania where he works as the Chief Commercial Officer of a multi-million dollar company.

> "If you want to learn presentation skills, public speaking or just simply uncover excellence hidden inside of you or your teams, **Akash Karia is the coach to go to**." — *Raju Mandhyan, TV show host, Expat Insights, Philippines*

> "Akash Karia is a fine public speaker who knows his subject very well. He has an immense understanding in what it takes for a successful presentation to pull through. **A rare talent who has much in store for you as an individual, and better yet, your organization**." — *Sherilyn Pang, Business Reporter, Capital TV, Malaysia*

> Voted as one of the "**10 online entrepreneurs you need to know in 2015**" by *The Expressive Leader*

Featured as one of the "**top 9 online presentations of 2014**" by *AuthorStream.com*

Akash is available for speaking engagements and flies from Tanzania. Contact him for coaching and training through his website: www.AkashKaria.com

YOUR FREE GIFT

As a way of saying thank you for your purchase, I'd like to offer you a free bonus package worth $297. This bonus package contains eBooks, videos and audiotapes on how to overcome procrastination, master the art of public speaking and triple your productivity. You can download the free bonus here: http://AkashKaria.com/FREE/

Made in the USA
Columbia, SC
18 October 2017